D0895279

BETHEL SEMINARY WEST
LIBRARY
6116 Arosa Street
San Diego, CA 92115-3902

PEOPLE
WHO MADE
A DIFFERENCE

MOTHER TERESA

Other titles in the
PEOPLE WHO MADE A DIFFERENCE
series include

Marie Curie
Father Damien
Mahatma Gandhi
Bob Geldof
Martin Luther King, Jr.

North American edition first published in 1990 by
Gareth Stevens Children's Books
1555 North RiverCenter Drive, Suite 201
Milwaukee, Wisconsin 53212, USA

First published in the United Kingdom in 1989. This edition
is abridged from the original published in 1988 by Exley
Publications Ltd. and written by Charlotte Gray. Copyright
© 1988 by Exley Publications. Additional end matter © 1990
by Gareth Stevens, Inc.

All rights reserved. No part of this book may be reproduced
in any form or by any means without permission in writing
from Gareth Stevens, Inc.

Library of Congress Cataloging-in-Publication Data

Gray, Charlotte, 1928-
  Mother Teresa: Servant to the world's suffering people / by
Charlotte Gray. — North American ed. / this edition written by
Susan Ullstein.
    p. cm. — (People who made a difference)
  Includes bibliographical references.
  Summary: A biography of the nun who founded the Missionary
Sisters and Brothers of Charity, gained wide recognition for her
work with the destitute and dying in Calcutta and elsewhere, and
was awarded the Nobel Peace Prize in 1979.
  ISBN 0-8368-0393-0
  1. Teresa, Mother, 1910- —Juvenile literature. 2. Nuns—India—
Calcutta—Biography—Juvenile literature. 3. Calcutta (India)—
Biography—Juvenile literature. [1. Teresa, Mother, 1910- . 2. Nuns.
3. Missionaries. 4. Missionaries of Charity.] I. Ullstein, Susan. II.
Title. III. Series.
BX4406.5.Z8G7   1990   271'.97—dc20
[B]   [92]   89-49750

For a free color catalog describing
Gareth Stevens' list of high-quality
children's books, call

1-800-341-3569 (USA) or
1-800-461-9120 (Canada)

PICTURE CREDITS
Camera Press — 28-29, 30, 31, 40, 42, 44,
46-47, 63; Croatian Catholic Mission — 6,
7 (both), 8, 10; Geoslides Photo Library
— 16-17, 21; Tom Hanley — 24, 33;
Photo Source Ltd. — 50 (below); Raghu
Rai — 25; Tom Redman — cover
illustration; Rex Features — 4; Frank
Spooner Pictures — 48, 51 (above); Teki
— 12, 13, 18, 19, 20, 23, 27, 36, 38, 39, 52,
54, 55; Universal Pictorial Press &
Agency Ltd. — 50 (top).
  Maps drawn by Geoffrey Pleasance.

The publishers have been unable to
contact either Teki or Raghu Rai; they
would much appreciate any information
which might help them to do so. They
would like to thank William Collins,
Sons & Co. Ltd. for permission to copy
illustrations from Desmond Doig's study
Mother Teresa — her people and her work.

Series conceived and edited by Helen Exley
Series editors, U.S.: Amy Bauman and Rhoda Irene Sherwood
Additional end matter, U.S.: Meredith Ackley
Research editor, U.S.: John D. Rateliff
Cover design: Kate Kriege

Printed in Hungary

1 2 3 4 5 6 7 8 9 96 95 94 93 92 91 90

PEOPLE
WHO MADE
A DIFFERENCE

Servant to the world's suffering people

MOTHER TERESA

Susan Ullstein's
adaptation of
the book by
Charlotte Gray

Gareth Stevens Children's Books
MILWAUKEE

The Nobel Peace Prize

On December 11, 1979, Mother Teresa went to Norway. She went to receive the greatest prize in the world — the Nobel Peace Prize. She stood in her blue and white sari in front of hundreds of important people. She spoke simply. She had no notes. She told them of the poverty and sadness in the world.

She accepted the prize of $190,000 not for herself but for the poor people of the world. She used the money to feed hungry people, to give homes to those who have nowhere to live, to give help to the sick and the dying. In fact, she received more than $190,000. There was not the usual Nobel banquet in 1979. The money that was saved on the banquet bought meals for fifteen thousand hungry people.

The Nobel Peace Prize is usually given to famous politicians, but Mother Teresa is not a politician. She is a nun, the mother superior of the Missionaries of Charity. She received the Nobel Peace Prize because her whole life has been devoted to loving and helping people.

"She embodies in herself compassion and love of humanity as few in history have done. . . . Her entire life has been a personification of service and compassion."
India's president,
N. S. Reddy,
presenting Mother Teresa with the Star of India

Opposite: Mother Teresa shows her Nobel Peace Prize certificate to the world. She received the award in Norway on December 17, 1979. At the time, the Washington Post *said,* "Occasionally the Norwegian Nobel Committee uses the prize to remind the world there is more than one kind of peace, and that politics is not the only way to pursue it."

5

This photo, taken in 1924, shows Agnes (seated), who would one day become Mother Teresa, with her brother, Lazar, and sister, Age. Agnes was fourteen and quite fashionably dressed. The photo was taken not long before Lazar left for a military academy. When Agnes left to become a nun, she wouldn't see Lazar again for thirty years.

6

Above, left: A rare early photo of Agnes, taken in September 1928, shortly before she left Albania to join the Loreto sisters. She would never see her mother or sister again.

Above: Agnes, age ten, with some friends from Skopje. Agnes is on the extreme left of the picture. She is wearing darker clothes than her friends because her father had died less than a year before.

Mother Teresa's early life

Mother Teresa was born on August 26, 1910, in Skopje, Albania. Her name was Agnes Gonxha Bojaxhiu. She was the youngest of three children. She had an older sister, Age, and an older brother, Lazar. It was an ordinary, happy family. They had a comfortable life. Agnes's father was a good businessman. He had his own company. He was full of life and very busy in politics. Agnes's mother was strict but very kind.

The family was Roman Catholic and very religious. They went to church

Sister Teresa (left) and another novice at the Loreto convent in Darjeeling in 1929 when she was eighteen. It shows the two nuns in the dark, heavy dress of nuns from Europe. Twenty years later, Sister Teresa would choose to be part of the Indian nation and would wear a sari.

almost every day. Agnes's mother taught her children to pray and to love and help other people. They often took food and money to the poor people of Skopje. Early in her life, Agnes learned the lesson of kindness from her mother.

Sadly, when Agnes was only nine, her father died. Suddenly, the Bojaxhiu family was very poor. At first, Agnes's mother was so sad that Age had to do everything. But later her mother opened a shop, and the business did well. Agnes had learned a second important lesson from her mother: when life is difficult, you must keep trying.

In 1924, Agnes and Age started going to a secondary school near their home. Agnes was very good at writing. Lazar thought that she would be a writer when she left school. But in 1928, when she was eighteen, Agnes decided differently. She wanted to become a nun. She wanted to be a missionary in India.

Agnes's mother understood her daughter's wish, although it was difficult for her. In those days, nuns did not go home to visit their families. If Agnes went to India, her family would probably never see her again. True enough, when Agnes said good-bye to her family, it was the last time she would see her mother and her sister. She didn't see her brother Lazar again until 1960.

Agnes becomes a nun

The family priest in Skopje told Agnes about the Sisters of Loreto who worked in Bengal in India. They were Irish nuns. Agnes wrote to them, and they asked her to go to France. They wanted her to meet the mother superior of the Sisters of Loreto in Paris.

And so, at the age of eighteen, Agnes left her family and went to Paris. Her

Sister Teresa (top right) in May 1937, just after she had taken her final vows. She had just been appointed principal of St. Mary's School at Entally, Calcutta. One of the other sisters described her as "delicate," — and no one would have guessed that eleven years later she would leave the convent to serve "the poorest of the poor."

meeting with the mother superior went well. Agnes was sent to Dublin, Ireland. There she began her training as a nun. She also had to learn English.

The "Little Way"

On December 1, 1928, after six weeks in Dublin, Agnes began the long journey by ship to India. She traveled with another girl who also wanted to become a nun. They finally arrived in Calcutta on January 6, 1929.

It takes a young woman many years to become a nun. She must be sure that this is the life she really wants because it will be forever. First, a woman becomes a novice. Then she must wait several years before she can take her final vows and become a nun.

On May 23, 1929, Agnes became a novice. Every novice chooses a new name for herself. Agnes chose *Teresa*, after Saint Thérèse of Lisieux, France. Saint Thérèse had taught that people can serve God by doing the simplest jobs gladly. Saint Thérèse called this her "Little Way." Agnes (now Sister Teresa) was very happy to follow in that way.

Sister Teresa was sent to the Loreto convent in Darjeeling, in the foothills of the Himalaya Mountains. She taught in the school there and worked in the hospital. In Darjeeling, she saw for the first time the terrible poverty of many Indians. She worked hard both at the hospital and the school, following Saint Thérèse's "Little Way."

Six years later, May 24, 1931, Sister Teresa took her first vows as a nun. She went back to Calcutta to teach in the school at Entally, a poor part of the city. There were two Loreto schools at Entally. There was a boarding school for the children of rich parents and a day school, Saint Mary's, for the children of poor parents. The poor children were taught in Bengali, not English. Sister Teresa taught history and geography. She was a good teacher. She enjoyed her work, and it showed. Her pupils loved her.

Six years later, in 1937, Sister Teresa took her final vows of poverty, chastity, and obedience. From now on she could have no money or possessions of her own. She could not marry, and she had

The front gate of the Entally Convent of the Sisters of Loreto. Sister Teresa spent over eleven peaceful years here, while World War II was being fought and India was trying to free itself from British rule. Although it was peaceful and quiet in the convent, the world outside the gates was filled with noisy, dirty slums in which poor people lived.

to obey the laws of the Roman Catholic church and the pope. Sister Teresa was finally a nun. She soon became principal of Saint Mary's School at Entally.

In those days, strict rules kept nuns inside their convents. They hardly ever went outside. If they did, they usually went in cars with other nuns. They saw little of the lives of the ordinary people who lived in India.

Sister Teresa was a very good teacher. She was so good that she soon began to teach at another local school, Saint Teresa's, as well as at Saint Mary's.

But Saint Teresa's School was not inside the Loreto convent. Sister Teresa had to walk beyond the convent gates to teach there. During these walks, she saw

again the terrible poverty of many Indian people, and she could not forget it.

Violence and change

Sister Teresa lived and worked for almost twenty years in the Loreto convent in Calcutta. People who knew her during those years remember her as an ordinary nun. Some even say she did not seem to be very strong. But they were wrong. They had no idea how much this little nun with the big heart could do.

During those twenty years, life inside the convent was calm and quiet. But outside, India was changing. With the change came violence. During the 1930s, Mahatma Gandhi was working hard to help the poor people of his country in a

The roofs of Motijhil (or "Pearl Lake"), the slum just outside the peaceful gardens of the convent. Girls from Sister Teresa's school worked hard to help the poor in Motijhil, but, because of the rules of the convent, the nuns were not allowed outside to join them.

nonviolent way. But then World War II began, and Calcutta was bombed by the Japanese. In 1943, there was a famine in Bengal, and five million people died because they had no food. Because of the war and the famine, many people came into Calcutta from the countryside. The streets were full of dying, hungry people. Sister Teresa and the nuns of Loreto helped the hungry and the sick as much as they could during the war, but they had to stay inside the convent.

For over two hundred years, the British had ruled India. In 1946, when they were getting ready to leave and let the country rule itself, violence broke out between Hindus and Muslims. There was fighting in the streets, and more than four thousand people were killed during only five days in August. By August 16, 1946, the children at the Loreto convent were very hungry, but there was no food left. It was very dangerous to leave the convent, but Sister Teresa had to get food for her children. So she went. She saw some terrible things. There were dead bodies everywhere. Some soldiers stopped Sister Teresa. They told her to go back to the convent immediately.

"But I must get some food for my children!" she said. "I have three hundred girls with nothing to eat."

And so the soldiers helped her. They found rice for the children. Then they

"She constantly found herself watching others go out to do the very work which she herself longed to do more than anything else. From her window in the convent she could see the misery of the Motijhil slums, stretching away beyond the trim lawns and tidy buildings of the Loreto property. It seemed that the only way to reach the poorest of the poor was to work outside the convent."
David Porter, in Mother Teresa: The Early Years

took Sister Teresa back to the convent. August 16, 1946, would later be called "The Day of the Great Killing."

On that day, Sister Teresa showed what she could do. When people need her help, she helps them — although the job seems impossible. Others' needs always come before her own safety.

Inspiration Day

In September 1946, Sister Teresa went to Darjeeling. All the Loreto nuns from Calcutta spent a little time in Darjeeling each year. It was a time for rest and prayer in the cool air of the mountains.

On September 10, 1946, something happened to Sister Teresa on the journey there. It was a very important day, and Sister Teresa's followers now celebrate it each year as "Inspiration Day," the day the Missionaries of Charity began.

During the journey, Sister Teresa suddenly knew that God had a special job for her. She knew that he wanted her to live and work in the worst slums of Calcutta. He wanted her to help the poorest of the poor. Sister Teresa knew immediately that this work would be very important.

She also knew that it would not be easy. She had taken her final vows as a nun almost ten years before. She was the principal of a big school. She would have to leave the school, leave the convent,

The slums of Calcutta are some of the worst in the world. Calcutta is less than forty miles (64 kilometers) from the border with Bangladesh, the poorest country in the world, and it has a direct rail link to the Indian state of Bihar, one of the poorest and most heavily populated areas of India. Many poor people come to the big city to try to make a living there.

and go into the filthy slums of Calcutta. It was a huge step to have to take.

For a time she told no one about it. Then, when she went back to Calcutta, she talked to a priest, Father van Exem. She knew him well, and she trusted him. He was very surprised, but he said he would talk to the archbishop. Finally, at the end of 1946, Sister Teresa met the archbishop. She told him about her plan. He did not like it at all. He told her to wait for a whole year. During that year, she had to think and pray. She had to be sure that she had really understood what God was saying to her.

And so, Sister Teresa spent all of 1947 waiting. That was the year that India became independent from Great Britain. At the same time, Pakistan separated from India. India was for the Hindus; Pakistan was for the Muslims. It was a time of great violence, but inside the convent, Sister Teresa went on working hard as usual.

Leaving Loreto

For a long time, nothing happened. Then in July 1948, a letter arrived from the archbishop. It said that Sister Teresa could go and work outside the convent.

17

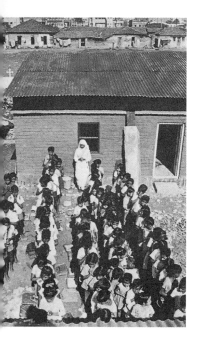

The courtyard in Motijhil, Calcutta, was where Mother Teresa opened her first school in December 1948. The school was her first and was started without any proper plans or equipment. Most of the work Mother Teresa does all over the world is started in this way.

But she was still a nun, and she had to keep her vows of poverty, chastity, and obedience. The archbishop gave her a year. During that year, she had to show that her plan would work. If, after a year, it had not worked, she would go back into the convent.

Sister Teresa wanted to start her new life immediately. But, on the other hand, it was difficult to leave the convent. After all, it had been her home for almost twenty years.

On August 16, 1948, Sister Teresa quietly left the Loreto convent at Entally for the last time. No one saw her go. She was not wearing the clothes of a European nun. Now she wore a blue and white Indian sari and a simple cross on her left shoulder.

Outside the walls

Sister Teresa went first to Patna, a city 240 miles (386 kilometers) from Calcutta. The Medical Mission Sisters ran the Hospital of the Holy Family there. Sister Teresa worked at their hospital for four months. She wanted to learn everything possible about how to nurse the poor.

Sister Teresa worked very hard. She learned about delivering babies, caring for the sick, and feeding the hungry. But above all else, she learned to understand the Indian people. Soon she became part of their lives.

The Medical Mission Sisters taught Sister Teresa many important lessons. For one thing, they said if she was going to take care of others, she must first take care of herself. She would have to eat healthy food and not miss meals. She would need to change and wash her sari once, if not twice, a day.

Sister Teresa always remembered the things the sisters taught her. Later, when she had young women working with her, she always made sure that they had enough food and rest.

In December 1948, Sister Teresa went back to Calcutta. For a few weeks, she stayed with the Little Sisters of the Poor. While there, she helped at Saint Joseph's, their home for old people. When she had decided exactly what to do, she went out into the slums for the first time. It was December 21, 1948. Sister Teresa had only five rupees, which the archbishop had given her.

The Missionaries of Charity now have more than 140 schools in India alone. In this picture of the first school yard in Motijhil, the sister at least has a blackboard and a table. At her first school, Mother Teresa scratched letters in the sand.

The work begins

Sister Teresa chose to begin work in Motijhil, one of the worst slums in Calcutta. She wanted to start a school for poor children. She knew that reading and writing were the keys to a better life.

She had known the priest in Motijhil, Father Julien Henry, for many years. He believed in Sister Teresa's plans to help the poor. He wanted to help her,

Father Julien Henry was Motijhil's local priest. He knew Mother Teresa well when she was principal at the Loreto convent. Father Henry had taken girls from her school to work among the people of the slums. He was one of the few priests who gave his support to Mother Teresa in the early years. He agreed with her idea that there was a great need to work right among the very poorest of the Bengali people.

although some of the priests thought she was foolish to think that one nun could help so many poor people.

But Sister Teresa believed that God would always help if the work was good. And so she prayed to God, and help came. She found a small hut with a courtyard, and she started her school. There were no tables, no chairs, no pens, no paper. In the beginning, Sister Teresa wrote letters and numbers in the earth. On the second day, someone gave her a chair, then a table, and her school grew.

Sister Teresa had begun her new life. In order to help the poor, she had to be poor. She had to live with the poor people to understand them. She had to live simply, like Jesus. She had started her first school with no money. She knew that God would help, and he did. And this is how the Missionaries of Charity have grown and grown. All over the world, when Mother Teresa and her followers need to help people, they trust God to help them.

The problems of the poor and the sick in India are very great. There are three million homeless people in Calcutta even today. At first, Sister Teresa worked alone. People wondered how one woman alone could help them. Sister Teresa began by doing small things. "Small things with great love" is how Mother Teresa describes her work.

From the beginning, in addition to running the school, Sister Teresa tried to help Calcutta's dying and homeless. One of the first people she helped was a dying man. He smelled so terrible that no one would go near him. She cleaned him and fed him. "Why are you doing this?" he asked her. "Because I love you," she answered. The man died soon after, but he died knowing that someone loved him. Since that time, Sister Teresa has helped more than forty-two thousand people on the streets of Calcutta.

From the very beginning of her work in Calcutta, Mother Teresa tried to help those who were dying on the streets. The task that Mother Teresa took on seemed to be endless because three million people are homeless in Calcutta. But, she says, the important thing is to begin and not be put off by how very difficult the task appears to be.

A new home

Soon the hut in Motijhil was too small. More and more people needed Sister

Teresa's help. She asked Father van Exem to help her again. She needed a bigger place.

Early in 1949, a man named Michael Gomes lent her the second floor of his house. Sister Teresa was very happy. She had an address at last — 14 Creek Lane. People could find her if they needed her.

Michael Gomes and his family helped Sister Teresa in many ways. They never asked for any rent for the second floor of the house. Gomes also gave Sister Teresa food and many other useful things. But he always says of that time, "We received. We did not give."

Gomes was glad to help Sister Teresa and to have her in his house. He often went with her to ask the owners of Calcutta's pharmacies for medicines. There were never enough for all the sick people who came to Sister Teresa for help. Once a pharmacist did not want to help. He went on with his work, but Sister Teresa and Gomes waited so patiently that, in the end, the druggist gave them plenty of useful medicines.

Gomes also gave Sister Teresa very good advice. Later on, in the 1950s (when Sister Teresa had become *Mother* Teresa), she started her first children's home, called Shishu Bhavan. The Indian government wanted to give her thirty-three rupees for each child at the home. At first, Mother Teresa was very pleased.

But Gomes told her to think again. Mother Teresa did. "No, thank you," she later said to the government. "If I take thirty-three rupees for each child, I'll have to spend exactly thirty-three rupees on each child. But often we don't need thirty-three rupees. We can use less." This is how Mother Teresa always works. She does not accept large amounts of money from any governments.

Gomes went on helping Mother Teresa for many, many years. Long after the days on Creek Lane, the Missionaries of Charity started a school called Protima Sen. It was for children who were in trouble with the police. The parents of these children had no control over them. Gomes was a teacher at this school. He wanted the children to learn Indian dancing. At first, Mother Teresa did not like the idea. But when she saw the children dancing, she was very pleased.

Sister Teresa worked from morning to night. There was so much to do. There were never enough hours in the day. But Sister Teresa felt that this was only the beginning, and she was right.

Sister Agnes, the first helper to join Mother Teresa in 1949: "I was one of her students at Entally and have known her since I was nine years old." Small, quiet, and shy, Sister Agnes handled much of the organization of the Missionaries of Charity in India.

The first helpers

Soon some of Sister Teresa's pupils from the Loreto convent came to help her. The first was Subashini Das. She came to Sister Teresa on March 19, 1949. Her family was rich, but she wanted to help

23

The first novices to join Sister Teresa cared for children without parents and children left in the streets. At first, the novices found it hard to look after the one or two extra babies that arrived every day, but now the work has grown, and sixty or seventy children are rescued every day in Calcutta alone.

Sister Teresa with her work. She became the first Missionary of Charity. She chose Sister Teresa's original name, Agnes, as her religious name.

In a few weeks, Magdalena — another Loreto pupil — arrived. Her family did not want her to work with Sister Teresa. They wanted her to go on studying because she was very bright. But Magdalena stayed with Sister Teresa and became Sister Gertrude. After two years, her family accepted her decision. She did go on with her studies and became a doctor. Years later, Sister Teresa sent her to Yemen to look after the sick there.

A third young woman arrived and became Sister Dorothy. Then a fourth came. She became known as Sister Margaret Mary. Later, in 1955, Charur Ma, the cook from the Loreto convent, went to work at Sister Teresa's children's home, Shishu Bhavan.

During her first year away from the Loreto convent, Sister Teresa and her four helpers worked very hard. They fed the hungry. They asked all the Christians in Calcutta not to throw away any food. Then the sisters collected the food and gave it to the hungry.

The sisters went on running the school at Motijhil. They took in unwanted babies and children. Every day they found two or three. Some of the children died, but many lived.

The sisters also helped the sick and the dying. They found one woman who was too weak to help herself lying in the street. Sister Teresa took her to the nearest hospital. They could not cure her. They wanted the old woman taken away. But Sister Teresa did not go away. In the end, the hospital gave the old woman a bed. "We cannot let a child of God die like an animal," Mother Teresa said later.

The number of people living on the second floor at 14 Creek Lane grew and

Michael Gomes lent part of his house on Creek Lane to Mother Teresa and her first helpers. Eventually there were nearly thirty of them living in a large upstairs room and doing their laundry on the roof. Michael Gomes thought it was a blessing to have Mother Teresa living in his house.

grew. It became so crowded that they had to build extra rooms on the roof. Even though it was crowded, 14 Creek Lane was a very happy place. Michael Gomes remembers that there was a lot of laughter. The sisters used to play games when they were not working or praying. When Sister Agnes looks back to those early days, she remembers the happy times as well as the hard work.

Sister Teresa worked harder than anyone. People were surprised by how strong this frail-looking woman was. She often worked twenty-one hours a day. In the morning, she left the house to work in the slums. When she was out, she did not eat or drink anything. When she went back to Creek Lane in the evening, she had more work to do. She took great care of the sisters. She shared all the jobs. She *never* asked others to do jobs she would not do herself.

Sometimes, Sister Teresa worked too hard. Then she would have to go to bed. Once when she was ill, she got a note from a man who was a Hindu. In those days, many Hindus were against Sister Teresa. They did not like her Christian religion. But this man knew that Sister Teresa was doing wonderful work. In his note he said that he had prayed to the Hindu goddess Kali to cure her.

In 1950, Sister Teresa took on Indian citizenship. She was an Indian at last.

Opposite: The most important thing in Mother Teresa's life is her religion. "My life is devoted to Christ," she says. "It is for him that I breathe and see. I can't bear the pain when people call me a social worker. Had I been in social work, I would have left it long ago."

The Missionaries of Charity

At the end of Sister Teresa's first year away from the Loreto convent, the archbishop of Calcutta realized that she and her fellow nuns were doing wonderful work. This was work no one had done before. The sisters had shown that Sister Teresa's plan could work. Everyone wanted Sister Teresa to go on.

By the end of 1950, Sister Teresa already had twelve helpers. Their numbers grew steadily. By 1988, there would be over three thousand sisters and novices. Worldwide, there would be seventy thousand Co-Workers.

And so Sister Teresa wrote the Rule of the Missionaries of Charity. To the usual vows of poverty, chastity, and obedience, she added another promise. The sisters had to serve the poorest of the poor all over the world. On October 7, 1950, Pope Pius XII gave his support to the Missionaries of Charity. Sister Teresa, once a teacher and the principal of a girls'

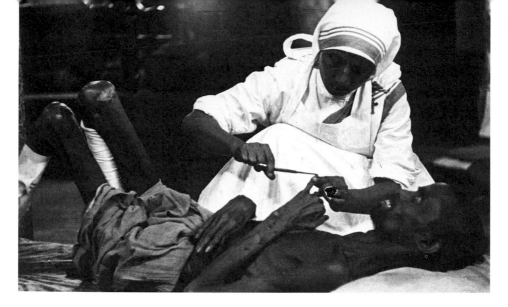

This nun is cutting a dying man's fingernails and cleaning his sores. The sisters have always deliberately chosen what most people would feel are the worst jobs. For example, when civil war broke out in 1971 in East Pakistan (now called Bangladesh), more than one million people escaped into India. Thousands of aid workers flew into the country to help. The Missionaries of Charity did the most basic jobs, such as cleaning and burying the dead.

school, was now the mother superior of the Missionaries of Charity. She and her sisters chose to do the worst jobs. They chose to help the people that no one else wanted to help.

Mother Teresa's Christian faith is the center of her life. And so she wants to "live Jesus's love for people." She wants to help people, but above all else, she wants to love them.

The motherhouse

In 1952, there were twenty-eight Missionary Sisters of Charity living at the Gomes house on Creek Lane. By this time, the second floor was finally getting too crowded. The sisters needed a new house, but they had very little money. Father Henry and Father van Exem helped Mother Teresa in her search for a bigger house.

At that time, there was still much trouble between the Hindus and the Muslims in India. Many Muslims were leaving India and going to live in Pakistan. One of Father van Exem's friends was a Muslim. This man was also planning to leave India. He was a rich man, and he had a huge house. He told Father van Exem that he wanted to give Mother Teresa his house. "I got the house from God," the man said. "I give it back to him now."

So 54A Lower Circular Road, Calcutta, became the motherhouse of the Missionary Sisters of Charity. And it was all because of the kindness of a Muslim to a Christian. The sisters live there to this day. It is a very special place — a very calm, peaceful place.

The Missionaries of Charity take a vow of poverty that states that they can own only a few things. No sister is allowed to receive gifts for herself, and she is not allowed to read books unless they are about religion. The umbrellas below are shared by all the sisters.

Shishu Bhavan

If the motherhouse of the order is a quiet place, the working headquarters of the Missionaries of Charity at Shishu Bhavan is not. It is a busy, noisy place. Many people come every day for help, for medicines, and for food.

Today six thousand people are fed every day at Shishu Bhavan. The food is cooked in big pans over open fires in the courtyard. Everyone who comes is treated with great care and love, but babies and children get an extra special welcome. Some of the babies weigh less than thirty-six ounces (about one kilogram). Some of the children are so ill that they die, but many get better and live healthy lives. The sisters wash them, feed them, and give them medicine. They play with them, and teach them to read and write. But, above all, they give them love and kindness. They let the children know that they are wanted. Some of the children are later adopted by families from all over the world.

Stories of caring

There are many wonderful stories about the children who have been helped by the Missionaries of Charity. One little boy had no one in the world. His grandmother, who had looked after him, had died. He went to Shishu Bhavan. The sisters took care of him. If anyone asked him what he wanted to be when he grew up, he always said, "I'm going to be Mother Teresa." Although he could not be Mother Teresa, he did become a priest and now works to help the poor.

The sisters often pay for one or two children from a large family to go to school. When the children grow older, they can then get jobs. They then look after the other people in their families. If the sisters did not help these children, the whole family would always be poor. The children would never have enough food to eat or enough beds to sleep in.

"We must never think any one of us is indispensable. God has ways and means. He may allow everything to go upside down in the hands of a very talented and capable sister. God sees only her love. She may exhaust herself, even kill herself with work, but unless her work is interwoven with love, it is useless."
Mother Teresa

Another story tells of a family of many children. The children's mother became sick and died. This left the oldest child, Rita, a girl of fourteen, to look after all her brothers and sisters. All of the children were very thin and hungry, but Rita was most worried about the youngest of her brothers. He was very ill. He was so weak that he never moved or cried He certainly never smiled. Finally, Rita took her brothers and sisters to Mother Teresa and the other nuns for help.

A newspaper reporter heard about the children. He wrote a news story about

The sisters started feeding small groups of starving people. The numbers grew rapidly, but so did the donations and gifts of food. Every day now, the sisters feed six thousand people from the worst slum areas of the world.

"I have never met anyone more memorable. I have known people to burst into tears when she goes, though it was only from a tea party where their acquaintance with her amounted to no more than receiving her smile."

Malcolm Muggeridge, in Something Beautiful for God

"I believe no other philosopher or humanist has such a lively sense of the humanity and the value of every human being."

Sandro Bordignon, French journalist

the children and how the sisters helped them. Many of the newspaper's readers sent money for the children — seven thousand rupees in all. Mother Teresa immediately put five thousand rupees in the bank. This was for Rita when she got married. It was her dowry — the money or land that is given to a woman's husband when they marry. Mother Teresa used the other two thousand rupees for the other children.

At first, the reporter was angry with Mother Teresa. He said the money was for *all* the children in the family. But Mother Teresa was right. She knew the Indian way of life. Without the five thousand rupees, Rita would have no dowry. Without that, she would never find a husband and marry. She would never know a better life.

Mother Teresa found another small boy sitting under a tree. He had run away from his cruel uncle and aunt (his parents were dead). Mother Teresa took the boy to Shishu Bhavan. He went to school and did very well. But he was always sad and alone.

One day, the boy told Mother Teresa that he wanted to get married. She thought that he was too young to marry, but she wanted to help. So she bought him a small piece of land. He built a house on it. Soon after, he got married and was very happy.

Mother Teresa holds and protects a young child, one of so many who are helped. Each day, she and her fellow nuns rise at 4:40 A.M., pray, wash, love, serve, and then pray, work, love, and serve again. Day after day. Year after year. In different ways, she says many thousands of times, "Give until it hurts."

When Shishu Bhavan first opened, people came to Mother Teresa. They wanted the children of Shishu Bhavan to be their servants. They thought that the poor children of Shishu Bhavan would work in their homes for very little money. Mother Teresa was angry with them. She sent them away. "If you cannot afford to pay a servant good money, you should not have a servant," she said.

Sealdah Station

The sisters of the Missionaries of Charity went all over Calcutta to help the sick. One very sad place was Sealdah Station. Although it was just a railroad station, thousands of people actually lived there. They ate, cooked, slept, and died there.

The Indian government tried to help. They moved many families to new homes in the country. But every day, more people arrived at Sealdah Station. For more than twenty years, between 3,000 and 4,000 poor people have arrived in Calcutta every day. If there is a famine, more come. They hope to find a better life in the city. Often, life in the city is worse than the life they have left.

The sisters did as much as they could to help these people. If the people could cook their own food, the sisters gave them wheat and soya, which is a high-protein product made from soybeans. This did not taste as good as rice, but it kept the people alive. For those people who could not cook for themselves, the sisters cooked the wheat and soya for them in big pans. They gave medicine to the sick. They took many of the children to Shishu Bhavan for help. But every day, more people needed their help.

Life on the streets

In the 1950s, there were between six million and eight million people in

Opposite: The sisters started work among the homeless at Sealdah Station. The big railroad stations have always been shelters for those who have nowhere else to live. Nowadays they are looked after by the Missionary Brothers of Charity.

Calcutta. At least 200 thousand of these people lived on the streets. With no other home, they cooked, ate, slept, washed, and died on the streets of the city.

Mother Teresa and her Sisters of Charity tried hard to help these people. They found many lying sick in the streets. The nuns would take these people to a nearby hospital. But Calcutta hospitals were so crowded that they could only take in people who could be cured. Many of the people that the sisters found were so ill that they would soon die. So Mother Teresa rented a room and took some of them there. They were often very dirty and smelly. It was difficult to go near them. But Mother Teresa and her helpers did not think about the smell and the dirt. They wanted to help. They wanted these people to know God's love.

Nirmal Hriday

Every day, Mother Teresa and the other nuns found more desperate people. The rented room was not big enough. So Mother Teresa went to the government. She asked them to give her a house or a hut — anywhere. Finally, a man who worked for the government told her about a building near the Temple of Kali, the Hindu goddess after whom Calcutta is named. The building had not been used for years. It was very dirty. But it

Even the Indian government doesn't know how many people live in Calcutta. In 1980, there were nine million; today there are probably nearer twenty million. No matter how many people the sisters are able to help, there are always others, like this man who died alone on the streets.

was large, and it had gas and electricity. The man said that Mother Teresa could use the building. She was very happy. That day, the sisters began to clean the building. After a week of hard work, the building was clean, and the first people moved in. It was called Nirmal Hriday, which means "place of the pure heart."

The people who come to Nirmal Hriday have no hope. They cannot be cured, so no hospital will take them. But at Nirmal Hriday, people are cared for until they die. It does not matter who they are — young, old, Hindu, Christian, Muslim — everyone is welcome.

At first, the Hindu priests from the nearby Temple of Kali were against

This picture shows why no one knows how many people there are in Calcutta. Thousands of people wash, eat, live, and die on the streets of Calcutta.

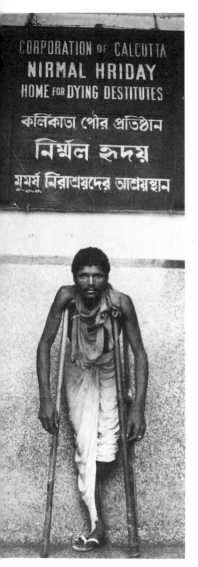

CORPORATION OF CALCUTTA
NIRMAL HRIDAY
HOME FOR DYING DESTITUTES

কলিকাতা পৌর প্রতিষ্ঠান

নির্মল হৃদয়

মুমূর্ষ নিরাশ্রয়দের আশ্রয়স্থান

Mother Teresa accepted this building, now called Nirmal Hriday, in 1952. The people who come here are dying and have nowhere to go. Crowded Calcutta hospitals cannot take people who cannot be cured.

Mother Teresa and the Missionaries of Charity. They did not like the Christian religion. Then one of the Hindu priests became ill. He could not be cured, so no hospital in Calcutta would take him in. But Mother Teresa did. The sisters at Nirmal Hriday cared for him until he died. After that, the Hindu priests began to think differently about Mother Teresa and the Missionaries of Charity.

But that did not end Mother Teresa's problems. Some Hindu men came to see her. They were afraid of her and her religion, too. They wanted her to leave Nirmal Hriday. When they saw what the Missionaries of Charity were doing, they also thought differently. They weren't willing to do her work, but later, one of them told the others that if their mothers, sisters, and daughters would do the work, he would stop Mother Teresa. But he knew that those women never would. And so Mother Teresa stayed.

Nirmal Hriday could be a sad and terrible place, but it is not. There is a lot of laughter there. The sisters are happy in their work. They do each of their jobs gladly. They feed the people who cannot feed themselves. They hold the hands of those who are afraid or in great pain. Through all they do, they try to show God's love to other people.

Many ordinary people go to Nirmal Hriday. Some of these people are visitors. They bring gifts — grapes, sweets, cigarettes — anything that will give comfort to the dying. Others come to help the sisters with the feeding, washing, cleaning, and cooking.

And even the desperate people who come to Nirmal Hriday for help often help each other. Charubala is one example. Mother Teresa found her on the streets of Calcutta when she was very old and sick. She could not walk or do much of anything else for herself. The sisters washed her and cared for her. The woman in the bed next to Charubala could not feed herself. Charubala could still use her hands, so she fed the woman. She also used to sing beautiful songs to the other people.

To the sisters, it is important that the people who die in their hospital know that they are loved. In the 1960s, Mother Teresa said, "In these twenty years of work among the people, I have come to realize that being unwanted is the worst disease any man or woman can have." This is still true today.

Becoming a Sister of Charity

The young women who become Sisters of Charity have to be totally sure it is what they want. It takes nine years to become a sister. Most of the women begin as a "come-and-see," as Mother Teresa calls them. At first, the women

"Today, talking about the poor is in fashion. Knowing, loving, and serving the poor is quite a different matter."
Mother Teresa

work at Shishu Bhavan, Nirmal Hriday, and on Calcutta's streets. After a year, if they still want to go on, they become novices and start their training. They choose their religious names and study the Roman Catholic religion. They must also learn English if they do not know it. At the same time, they go on helping the poorest of the poor. Each Thursday, the sisters pray and rest. They study their religion and clean the convent.

For the first two years, the novices wear white saris. Then, at the beginning of their third year, they take their first vows and start to wear blue and white saris. They take more vows at the end of the fourth and sixth years. In the sixth year, the sisters go to Calcutta or Rome for a year of religious study. Only after that can they take their final vows as Missionary Sisters of Charity.

The vow of poverty

Mother Teresa's Missionaries of Charity have very few possessions. For clothing, each sister is given three saris — one to wear, one to wash, and one to mend. Each of the sisters also has a pair of sandals, two sets of underclothes, a small cross which she wears on her left shoulder, and a rosary for prayer. In the colder countries, each sister may also have a woolen jacket. Finally, each has a spoon, a plate, a bag, and a prayer book.

"Nowadays, we have found medicine for leprosy, and lepers can be cured. . . . For all kinds of diseases there are medicines and cures. But for being unwanted, [unless] there are willing hands to serve and there's a loving heart to love, I don't think this terrible disease can ever be cured."
Mother Teresa

Opposite: Mother Teresa started her work with the dying by picking up one person. The sisters now run eighty hospices and care for over thirteen thousand dying people each year. To the sisters, it is important that each person dies with the feeling of being loved.

43

The sisters start each day by praying together. They return at lunchtime and at night to eat, pray, and sleep. There is much laughter in the houses, and the sisters all follow Mother Teresa's motto: "Together." This sense of sharing, of working and living together, helps to give the sisters the strength to do the work they do. Although they see a lot of suffering, the sisters always have a bright and cheerful look on their faces.

Mother Teresa has said, "In order to understand poverty, we must be poor." She means it. The sisters have simple lives. They cannot receive letters or gifts from their friends or their families. They never go to the movies, the theater, or parties. They can read only religious books. Their lives are given to God.

Life at the motherhouse

The day begins very early at 54A Lower Circular Road in Calcutta. A bell rings at

4:40 in the morning. The sisters get up and go to the chapel. Outside the chapel is a list of people from all over the world who have asked the sisters to pray for them. Inside the chapel, a crucifix hangs above the altar. The words "I thirst" are above the crucifix to remind the sisters of Jesus' words, "I was thirsty and you gave me to drink; . . . as long as you did it for one of these, the least of my brethren, you did it for me."

Prayers end, and it is breakfast time. After that, the sisters get ready to go out into the city. Each packs a bottle of water in her bag in case she gets thirsty. The sisters never take food or drink from anyone. They travel in pairs and walk, if possible, rather than take a bus. As they walk, they pray, using their rosaries.

At noon, the sisters come back to the motherhouse. They eat lunch and wash up. They also wash yesterday's saris in buckets in the courtyard. People have often wanted to give the sisters washing machines, but Mother Teresa always smiles, saying, "No, thank you. We don't need washing machines." Then they sleep for half an hour before it is time for prayer again. At two o'clock, they go out into the streets again. It seems that they do more than two days' work in one day.

At six o'clock, the sisters come home. They go to the chapel to pray and then they have dinner. After dinner they can

"Her and the Sisters' and Brothers' identification with the poor among whom they live is no mere figure of speech. They eat the same food, wear the same clothes, possess as little, are not permitted to have a fan . . . in Bengal's sweltering heat."
Malcolm Muggeridge, in
Something Beautiful
for God

45

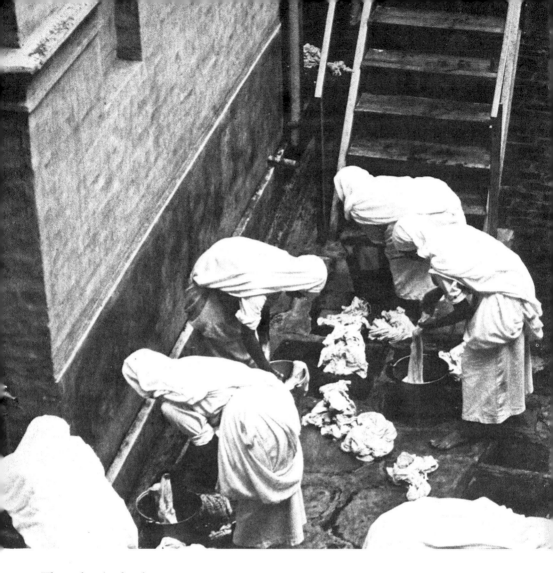

Thursday is the day when the Calcutta novices go out to run the clinics and schools so that the sisters can stay home to study, mend their saris, and clean the convent. The sisters use tin buckets to wash their clothes.

read or talk about their day. At the very end of the day, they go to the chapel again for prayers. By ten o'clock, almost everyone is asleep. But not Mother Teresa. She works late into the night. Someone once asked her how she could live with so little sleep. Mother Teresa laughed and said, "I sleep fast!"

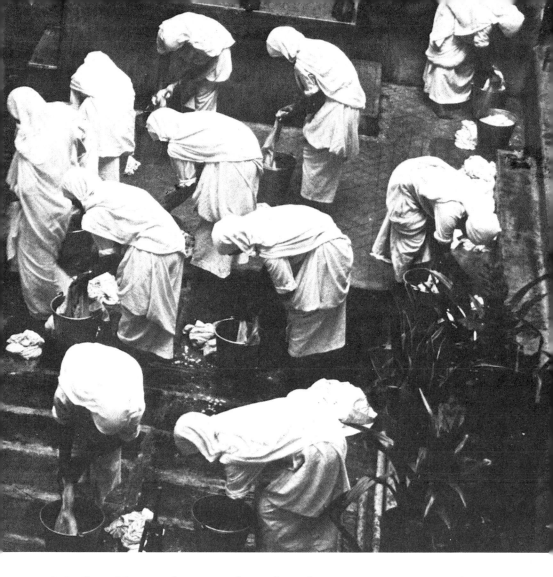

Mother Teresa knows that the sisters have difficult lives. They work hard, and they see terrible, sad things every day. She believes that the strength of the Missionaries of Charity comes from sharing. She does everything she can to give the sisters a sense of community. For this reason, Mother Teresa made a

In more recent years, Mother Teresa has had to start using the telephone. She could no longer visit every house every two years. It seems to have made little difference to the smooth running of the houses. She explains their tasks so well that the sisters hardly ever need to ask her advice before making a decision.

"The rich, when they come to her, are liable to leave a little less rich, which she considers as conferring a great favor on them. On the other hand, she has never accepted any government grants in connection with her medical and social work. This, she says, . . . would involve keeping accounts. I quite see her point."

Malcolm Muggeridge, in
Something Beautiful
for God

rule that, if possible, the sisters must always sleep at the motherhouse. So they take turns staying at Shishu Bhavan, but helpers look after Nirmal Hriday at night. "Everything together," Mother Teresa says. She takes good care of them.

Gifts of love

Mother Teresa never worried about money. She always said that help comes when it is needed, and it always has. Today, she receives money from all over the world — from the rich and the poor.

People do not only give money. In 1964, Pope Paul VI visited India. When he left, he gave his car to Mother Teresa.

What could she do with a Rolls-Royce? Mother Teresa decided to sell the car. She held an auction and sold it to the person who bid the most money. This money also went to the poor.

In 1973, Mother Teresa was given a very large building that had been a factory. She called it Prem Daan, which means "gift of love." Many sick people live there now.

Waste not, want not

Mother Teresa believes strongly that nothing should be wasted. When she travels on an airplane, she always asks for the food that other passengers do not want. Later, she gives it to the hungry.

Some of the people who live at Prem Daan run a little workshop. There they make bags, mats, and other things from the coconut shells that litter the streets of Calcutta.

At Kidderpore, many people find work only when ships come to port. The sisters have found other work for the people. They collect waste paper from shops, offices, factories, anywhere, and the people make bags from it. The money made from selling the bags can make a great difference to poor families.

Missionary Brothers of Charity

In 1963, Mother Teresa welcomed the first brothers to the Missionaries of

BETHEL SEMINARY WEST LIBRARY
6116 Arosa Street
San Diego, CA 92115-3902

"She was outrageously brilliant. She made them [the journalists] laugh. . . . She understood that the moral ground she occupied gave her the right to march up to airlines and ask for a free ticket to Washington and, once she arrived, to ask to see the President of the United States knowing he dare not refuse her."

Bob Geldof, in his autobiography, Is That It?

Mother Teresa's fame spread. Ceremonies, such as one in London that called for her to read a prayer for peace (above), and meetings with important people, such as Prince Charles (right), happened more and more often. She received the Nobel Prize in 1979, but the awards she treasures most are those from India, her adopted country.

Charity. Like the sisters, they come from all over the world. Brother Andrew was the first. He had been a Jesuit priest, but he left the Jesuits to help Mother Teresa.

By 1975, 175 brothers ran ten houses in India and two in South Vietnam. The brothers do not look like priests. They wear ordinary clothes while working with sick, dying, and troubled people. Like the sisters, they treat desperate people with love and kindness. By 1988, there were 380 brothers. They now run ninety-one houses in thirty countries.

Work outside India

By the 1960s, Mother Teresa's Missionaries of Charity were all over

In September 1986, Mother Teresa delivered a message to the Ninth International Congress on the Family in Paris.

"I felt I had no business sitting beside this tiny giant. But there was nothing other-worldly or divine about her."
  Bob Geldof, in his autobiography, Is That It?

Mother Teresa stands with Brother Andrew, then general servant of the Missionary Brothers of Charity. This order was founded in 1963. In 1970, there were only 86 brothers. In 1988, 380 brothers ran ninety-one homes in thirty countries.

India. They ran hospitals, schools, houses, and clinics. But Mother Teresa knew that desperate people lived in countries throughout the world.

In 1965, Pope Paul VI let the Missionaries of Charity begin work outside India for the first time. Soon, Mother Teresa had opened one house in Venezuela and another in Ceylon (now Sri Lanka). In 1968, she visited Rome. Some people were surprised when Mother Teresa decided to work in Rome. But Mother Teresa knows that poverty is not the same in every country. In India, poverty can be found everywhere. But poverty also exists in other countries, although it cannot be seen as easily.

The Barrachi

Mother Teresa found the Barrachi on the edge of Rome. In the Barrachi, poor people live in shacks because they cannot afford to buy or rent houses in the city. There they build shacks out of old boxes, oil cans, wood, and other items that people have thrown away. Despite the poverty, the Barrachi is home to many.

The sisters do what they can to help. A community building stands in the center of the Barrachi. In it, the sisters run a day-care center. From there, they also go into people's homes and help with cleaning, cooking, washing, or whatever else needs to be done.

All over the world

Through her travels, Mother Teresa has seen that every country has its problems. Since the 1960s, more and more of her houses have opened all over the world. Three hundred houses are now found in more than seventy countries on all continents of the world. There are houses in Peru, Northern Ireland, Papua New Guinea, Australia, France, Ethiopia, Spain, Chile, Panama, and Kenya.

It was in London and New York that Mother Teresa first saw the problems of drugs. Brothers and Sisters of Charity now work in both cities to help drug abusers. They also work with victims of the disease known as AIDS.

In the beginning, Mother Teresa tried to visit every house every two years. But today, the number of houses is so great that this is impossible. Still, the work goes on. Mother Teresa now uses the telephone a lot, and there is a special newspaper for all the Missionaries of Charity. It is called *Ek Dil*, which means "one heart" in Hindi.

Mobile clinics

From the beginning, a lot of people needed help. The sisters and brothers worked as hard as they could, but there were always more people in need.

In the early days, someone gave Mother Teresa $25,000. With that and

"Be kind to each other in your homes. Be kind to those who surround you. I prefer that you make mistakes in kindness rather than that you work miracles in unkindness. Often just for one word, one look, one quick action, and darkness fills the heart of the one we love."

Mother Teresa,
to the Co-Workers

"Someone will ask, 'What can I do to help?' Her response is always the same, a response that reveals the clarity of her vision. . . . 'Just begin, one, one, one,' she urges. 'Begin at home by saying something good to your child, to your husband, or to your wife. Begin by helping someone in need in your community, at work, or at school. Begin by making whatever you do something beautiful for God.'"

From an interview
with Mother Teresa,
from "Words to Love By."

Opposite: Leprosy
victims who live at
Titagarh and other
leprosy settlements make
paper bags and sandals
that can then be sold.
They also weave sheets
and saris for the sisters.

Mobile clinics allow the
sisters to reach patients
in many more areas.
They are particularly
useful in helping
victims of leprosy.

other gifts, she decided to make a truck
into a mobile clinic. Often, the people
who needed help the most could not
afford to travel to the sisters' ordinary
clinics. With the mobile clinics, the
sisters could go to them. Today, there are
670 mobile clinics. They help six million
people a year.

The mobile clinics go to a different
place each day. One often goes to
Kidderpore. The air in the city is very
dirty. The dust and smoke in it make
many people ill. Without help, some
children become blind. But the people of
Kidderpore have trouble seeing a doctor.
The people there are very poor because
there is often no work. Also, many of the
people in Kidderpore are Muslims.
Muslim women can see only women
doctors because their religion says so. So
Mother Teresa's mobile clinic is a great
help to these people.

Leprosy

Another large group of people needed
Mother Teresa's help — the people with
leprosy. In India today, four million
people suffer from leprosy. This disease
affects fifteen million people all over the
world. Although it can be cured now,
people still fear leprosy. In many places,
people who have leprosy must leave
their homes and their families. They
cannot get jobs. Other people will not go

near them. People suffering from this disease lead terrible lives.

In 1952, when Mother Teresa opened Nirmal Hriday, she said that victims of leprosy must not go there. But people with the disease heard about her wonderful work. Many came to Nirmal Hriday for help. Mother Teresa knew she had to do something for them.

By 1956, she had started eight leprosy centers in Calcutta. The sisters went from center to center in a bright blue truck. Then, in 1959, India's railroad company let Mother Teresa open a leprosy clinic at Titagarh. There, some of the worst victims could stay and be helped. Many victims came each day.

Mother Teresa also began a school for the children of leprosy victims. The children learn to look for signs of leprosy. This helps the sisters catch the disease early, when many people can be cured.

Slowly the people of Calcutta realized that leprosy could be cured. Signs appeared all over the city. They said, "Touch a leper with your love." Money was collected. In 1969, India's government gave Mother Teresa some land. It was in Asanol, two hundred miles (322 kilometers) from Calcutta. Called Shanti Nagar, meaning "town of peace," it became home to hundreds of leprosy victims and their families. Today it is a busy place, full of hope.

"I have never met anyone less sentimental . . . more down-to-earth. Thus, until [Mother Teresa] can accommodate her lepers in proper settlements where they can live useful, productive lives together, they still go out to beg in the streets of Calcutta if they want to. 'It's interesting for them,' she explained to me. If she happens to see them when they have come back, she will ask them how they have done."
Malcolm Muggeridge, in Something Beautiful for God

One woman, one world

And so the work of the Missionaries of Charity grows. Today, the order's two thousand sisters and novices and its four hundred brothers serve the entire world.

For her work, Mother Teresa has been given many honors: in 1971, the Pope John XXIII Peace Award and the John F. Kennedy International Award; in 1975, the Albert Schweitzer International Prize; in 1979, the Nobel Peace Prize; and in 1983, the Order of Merit from Queen Elizabeth II of Great Britain.

In September 1989, she went into the hospital with heart problems. That month, she received a pacemaker — a device that controls the heartbeat. The pacemaker will help Mother Teresa's heart do its work so that she can continue hers. Her life is nearing its end. But however long she may live, her ideas and her work will live past anyone's lifetime.

"Asked about the future of the congregation after her death she said, 'Let me die first, then God will provide. He will find someone more hopeless than I to do his work.'"

Mother Teresa, to a
Co-Worker

The Missionaries of Charity worldwide

The Missionaries of Charity are a rapidly growing religious order. They now have well over three hundred houses throughout the world, more than half of them outside India. They keep in touch through their newspaper, Ek Dil, which means "one heart" in Hindi. The order, which helps people with all kinds of problems, will soon begin work in the Soviet Union. The missionaries include seventy thousand Co-Workers. Co-Workers are people who wish to work with Mother Teresa but do not wish to join a religious order.

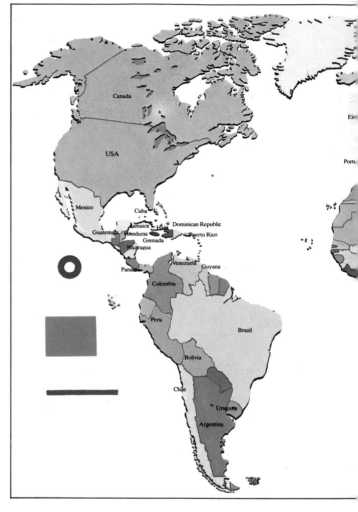

The houses around the world

B = Houses of Brothers (orders that are active in teaching, nursing, and ministering to others in the world)
C = Contemplative orders (groups that focus on prayer, meditation, and penance rather than work in the outside world)

Africa
Benin (2)
Burundi (2)
Cameroon (1)
Egypt (3)
Ethiopia (6, 1B)
Ghana (1B)
Kenya (2, 1B)
Madagascar (2B)
Mauritius (1, 1B)
Nigeria (1B)
Rwanda (2)
Seychelles (1)
Sudan (2)
Tanzania (3, 1B)

Asia (except India)
Bangladesh (7, 1B)
Hong Kong (2, 1B)
Japan (2, 1B)
Macau (1, 1B)
Nepal (1)
Pakistan (1)
Papua New Guinea (4)
Philippines (11, 2B)
Singapore (1, 1B)
South Korea (2, 6B)
Sri Lanka (1)
Taiwan (2, 1B)

Australia (7)

The Caribbean
Cuba (1)
Dominican Republic (2, 1B)
Grenada (1)
Haiti (4, 1B)
Jamaica (1)
Puerto Rico (1)

58

Europe
Austria (1)
Belgium (1)
East Germany (2)
Finland (1B)
France (2, 1B)
Great Britain (6, 1B)
Greece (1)
Ireland (Eire) (1)
Italy (12, 1B, 1C, 1BC)
Netherlands (1)
Poland (3)
Portugal (2)
Spain (2)
Sweden (1B)
West Germany (3)
Yugoslavia (2)

India (143, 46B, 1C)

Middle East
Israel (2)
Jordan (1)
Lebanon (1)
North Yemen (3)
Syria (2)

North and Central America
Canada (3)
El Salvador (1B)
Guatemala (1, 3B)
Honduras (2, 1B)
Mexico (4, 1B)
Nicaragua (1)
Panama (2)

United States (20, 7B, 4C)

South America
Argentina (2)
Bolivia (2, 1B)
Brazil (4, 1B)
Chile (2)
Colombia (4, 1B)
Guyana (1)
Peru (2, 1B)
Uruguay (1)
Venezuela (5)

To find out more . . .

Organizations

The following groups provide money, food, and other sources of aid to hungry, sick, and homeless people around the world. If you would like to know more about what they do or if you would like to help out, write to them at the addresses listed below. When you write, be sure to tell them exactly what you would like to know. Also include your name, address, and age.

American Friends Service Committee
Literature Resource Division
Africa Hunger and Development
1501 Cherry Street
Philadelphia, PA 19102

CARE
660 First Avenue
New York, NY 10016

Lutheran World Relief
390 Park Avenue South
New York, NY 10016

Missionaries of Charity
335 East 145th Street
New York, NY 10451

Oxfam America
115 Broadway
Boston, MA 02116

Save the Children Federation
Public Affairs
54 Wilton Road
Westport, CT 06880

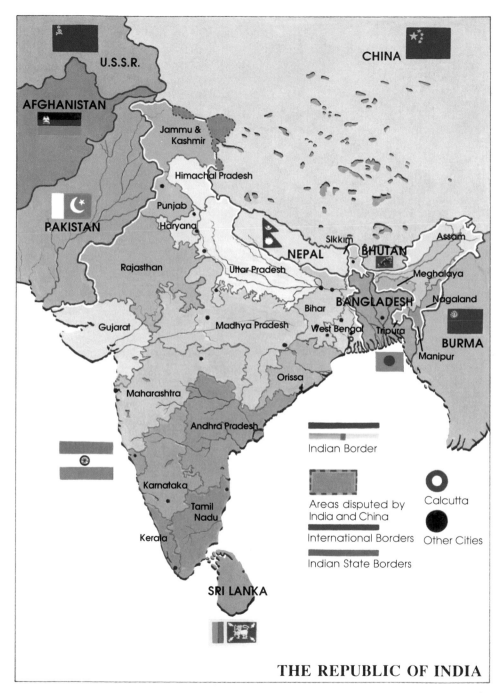

U.S.S.R.

AFGHANISTAN

CHINA

Jammu & Kashmir

Himachal Pradesh

PAKISTAN

Punjab

Haryana

Assam

Sikkim

BHUTAN

NEPAL

Meghalaya

Rajasthan

Uttar Pradesh

Nagaland

Bihar

BANGLADESH

Gujarat

Madhya Pradesh

West Bengal

Tripura

BURMA

Manipur

Orissa

Maharashtra

Andhra Pradesh

Indian Border

Karnataka

Areas disputed by
India and China

Calcutta

Tamil
Nadu

International Borders

Other Cities

Kerala

Indian State Borders

SRI LANKA

THE REPUBLIC OF INDIA

61

United Nations Children's Fund (UNICEF)
331 East 38th Street
New York, NY 10016

World Relief
Box WRC
Wheaton, IL 60189

World Vision
Public Relations Department
919 West Huntington Drive
Monrovia, CA 91016

Books

The following books provide further information about Mother
Teresa and India. If you would like to read more about these
subjects, check your local library or bookstore to see if they have
these books or if someone there can order them for you.

As They Saw India. Khanna (Auromere)
Living in India. Singh (Young Discovery Library)
Mother Teresa. Craig (David & Charles)
Mother Teresa: A Sister to the Poor. Giff (Viking Kestrel)
The Secret of the Drumstick Tree. Mook (Friends Press)
Take a Trip to India. Lye (Franklin Watts)

List of new words

auction
> A sale where people offer a price for an object they want to buy.
> The person who offers the highest price usually gets the object.

Bangladesh
> Area once called East Pakistan. It is located on the Bay of
> Bengal, between Burma and India. With help from India, it
> broke away from the rest of Pakistan and now rules itself.

Two members of the Missionaries of Charity carry donated food from a truck. There are 190 houses of Sisters and Brothers in India and 225 in other countries. If you would like to help, just write to them at the address listed on page 60. Please do not send cash to Calcutta. It is quite often stolen on the way.

banquet
   A meal with lots of good food and drink. It is usually held at an important occasion.

convent
   A building where Roman Catholic nuns live in a community.

Ek Dil
The Missionaries of Charity newspaper, which keeps all the houses in touch with each other. It means "one heart" in Hindi.

famine
A shortage of food that leaves people hungry for a long time.

headquarters
The main building or buildings of an organization.

Hindi
The language spoken by most of the people in India.

Hindu
A follower of Hinduism, the main religion of India. It is one of the five main religions of the world.

Kali
The Hindu goddess of destruction. She is usually depicted wearing a necklace of skulls.

leprosy
A disease that results in the loss of fingers and toes if it is not treated. Once, people with leprosy could not live with others.

Loreto
A place in Italy where Christians go to pray. It contains the house that the Virgin Mary is supposed to have lived in.

missionary
A person who travels to help others. Sometimes this person works in medicine or teaching or farming. A missionary usually represents a particular religious faith.

mobile clinic
A place for treating sick people that is driven to the patients.

motherhouse
The head convent or headquarters of an order of nuns.

Muslim
A follower of Islam, one of the five main religions. Islam is the main religion of Pakistan and Bangladesh.

Nirmal Hriday
"Place of the pure heart" in Hindi. It is the name given to the Missionaries of Charity house in Calcutta for dying people.

pope
Head of the Roman Catholic church.

religious order
A group of men and women who have vowed to devote their lives to religious aims.

rosary
A string of beads used by Roman Catholics to keep count of prayers to God and the Virgin Mary.

rupee
A unit of money used in India and Pakistan.

Saint Thérèse of the Child Jesus
A nun who died when she was twenty-four. Mother Teresa admired her and named herself after her.

sari
Traditional dress of Hindu women. It is a piece of cloth about 18 feet (6 meters) long, and about 3 feet (1 meter) wide.

Shanti Nagar
"Town of peace" in Hindi. It is the settlement for leprosy victims in Asanol, India.

Shishu Bhavan
The name of the headquarters of the Missionaries of Charity in Calcutta.

Sisters of Loreto
A religious order founded in 1609 by a woman from Ireland. The order has been working in Calcutta since 1841.

soya
The seed of a bean plant. It can be eaten.

Important dates

1910 **August 26** — Agnes Gonxha Bojaxhiu is born in Albania.

1928 **September 15** — Agnes leaves Albania for Ireland.
December 1 — Agnes goes by ship to India.

1931 Agnes takes her first vows. She becomes Sister Teresa and begins her teaching duties in Calcutta.

1937 Sister Teresa takes her final vows. She becomes principal of Saint Mary's School.

1946 **August 16** — "The Day of the Great Killing." Sister Teresa finds food for the children of the Loreto convent.
September 10 — "Inspiration Day." Sister Teresa believes God tells her to help "the poorest of the poor."

1947 India becomes independent.

1948 **August 16** — Sister Teresa leaves the Loreto convent.

1950 Pope Pius XII recognizes the Missionaries of Charity and Sister Teresa, as head of a motherhouse, becomes known as Mother Teresa.
Mother Teresa becomes a citizen of India.

1952	Mother Teresa opens Nirmal Hriday for dying people.
1953	The house at 54A Lower Circular Road, Calcutta, becomes the motherhouse of the Missionaries of Charity.
1955	Mother Teresa opens Shishu Bhavan, a shelter for people who are homeless.
1959	Mother Teresa opens Titagarh, a home for victims of leprosy.
1960	Mother Teresa visits the United States, Italy, England, and Germany; she sees her brother, Lazar, for the first time in thirty years.
1963	The Missionary Brothers of Charity begin work.
1965	Pope Paul VI lets the Missionaries of Charity work outside India. They open their first house outside India in Venezuela.
1971	**January 6** — Mother Teresa receives the Pope John XXIII Peace Award. **October 16** — Mother Teresa receives the John F. Kennedy International Award.
1975	Mother Teresa receives the Albert Schweitzer International Prize.
1979	Mother Teresa receives the Nobel Peace Prize.
1983	Queen Elizabeth II awards Mother Teresa the British Order of Merit.
1989	Mother Teresa experiences serious heart problems and is hospitalized.

Index

68